Mouth Like a Sailor

By

Maria Masington

This collection copyright © 2021 Maria Masington

All rights reserved by the author. For permission to reproduce any of the material in this volume, please contact the publisher via email: matt@parnilis.com

A PARNILIS MEDIA POETRY PRODUCTION

PARNILIS MEDIA
P.O. BOX 1461
MEDIA, PA 19063

ISBN: 978-1-954895-07-2

ACKNOWLEDGEMENTS

The following have been previously published:
November 22, 1963, *Wanderings*, 2013
Emanation, *Wanderings*, 2013
My mother wore a bikini in 1972, *Wanderings*, 2013
The New York Times, July 3, 1981, *The News Journal*, 2014
Lullaby, *Van Gogh's Ear*, 2014
The day you were born I grew fangs, *The News Journal*, 2014
My father was a paratrooper in Vietnam, *The Survivor's Review*, 2014
Sacrament, *Currents*, 2015
Old Wives' Tale, *Amore*, 2016
Radish Roses, *Broadkill Review*, 2017
Destiny of the Modern-Day Gladiola, *The Broadkill Review*, 2017
Circus Act, *Earth's Daughters*, 2018
Mouth like a Sailor, *Adanna* 2019
Charlotte's Adopted Son, *Delaware Bards Poetry Review*, 2019
1996 Man of the year, *New Page Ink*, 2020
Loaves and Fishes, *Sand Dune Poetry Anthology*, 2020
Statistics, *Never Forgotten 100 Poets Remember 9/11*, 2021
Survival of the Fittest, *Never Forgotten, 100 Poets Remember 9/11*, 2021
Aqua Zumba at the YMCA, *Gyroscope*, 2021
Rat with Furry Tails, *Markings*, 2021
Carnival Goldfish Boy, *The Broadkill Review*, 2021
Mantra, *Highland Park Poetry*, 2021
Storm Windows, *Raven Review*, 2021
Grandmother, *Delaware Literary Connection*, 2021
Snow White Walks Home from AA, pending *Gargoyle*, 2021

TABLE OF CONTENTS

Mermaids

Snow White Walks Home from AA	2
Clues	3
Sacrament	4
Destiny of the Modern-Day Gladiola	5
Loaves and Fish	6
The Wedgewood Nest	7
Rats with Furry Tails	8
Mantra	9

Christening the Ship

Circus Act	12
Lullaby	14
My mother wore a bikini in 1972	15
My father was a paratrooper in Vietnam	16
Eleven Weeks	18
1950 Western Union	19
Grandmother	20
Radish Roses	21

Cargo

The day you were born I grew fangs	24
Diameter of the Mouth	25
Carnival Goldfish Boy	26
Storm Windows	28
Checkmate	28
Charlotte's Adopted Son	30
His Time of the Month	32
Lactation	33

Anchored

I am turning 55 years old	36
Aqua Zumba at the YMCA	37
Math of the Mom & Pop Shop	38
Mouth like a Sailor	39
"Riding Mower $800 Good Working Condition"	40
Grand Slam	41
Terrain	42
Old Wives Tale	43

Distant Ports

November 22, 1963	46
New York Times July 3, 1981	47
Current Events	48
Emanation	49
1996 Man of the Year	50
Statistics of 9/11	51
Survival of the Fittest	52
Push Present	53

Dedication

Thanks to Matt Lake for taking a chance and making this book happen.

– to JoAnn Balingit for your encouragement at the very start.

– to Devon Miller-Duggan for *Friday Night Writes*, you're teachers, cheerleaders, champions all.

– to Panera Poets for your input and support, Billie Travalini for your time, Ramona for your life.

And as always, thank you to Bob Lutz, for absolutely everything…

MERMAIDS

Snow White Walks Home from AA

Leaves loosen their grip and float, dangle
like gems from her yellow skirt. Oak rubies and
birch emeralds cling to her black hair in a wispy
crown, like the lie of 'Happily Ever After.'

Maple whirlybirds fly to her feet. Detritus dusts
up like chipmunks racing her along the path,
circling her like reel-to-reel tapes of long-ago
conversations with witches, queens, and small men.

Mushrooms freckle the forest floor. Resentments
pop up again and again, betrayal and injustices,
real and imagined. She believes everything she thinks,
a tale where she is cast as dupe instead of darling.

She tries to remember their names, the Seven. She
knew them before the Fall. Happy, Doc, Bashful,
Sneezy, Restless, Irritable, and Discontented. Miners
of seven deadly sins, *we dig, dig, heigh ho, heigh ho.*

She loses focus, her eyes jewelers' loupes,
magnifying and misinterpreting outdated
conversations, tiny slights and unintended harms,
rewriting history to suit her mood and attitude.

Acorns plunk like cocktail olives onto the trampoline
of the decaying forest floor. Squirrels trapeze above
her head, chiding her to face the girl in the mirror,
chattering that she should stop biting the poison apple.

Step-by-step, foliage crumbles under high yellow heels,
powdery remnants of resentment in the woods' musty air.
A mile in her sober shoes, flakes of jewel-toned leaves
speckle her silk stockings and anger clings to her soles.

Clues

It may have been Colonel Mustard,
or Mister Green.
For all she knew, it could
have been Miss Scarlett,
or her weird uncle,
or one of her brothers.

Maybe it was with the rope,
or the pipe, or the candlestick,
or an adult body,
or a Coke bottle.

In the conservatory, the library,
or perhaps the billiard room.
Or in the family camper,
or her own canopy bed.

She wasn't sure.
She had no face and few details,
but her body had instincts,
visceral, foggy memories of
things she'd always known.

If only she could roll the dice, guess,
and her mother, or father, or sister,
would nod and validate her reality

when she suggested
that it was Professor Plum
with the dagger,
in the ballroom.

Sacrament

"Bless me Father, for I have sinned.
It has been one week since my last confession."

A job he shortened to a number system,
explained to children on book markers.

Each sin assigned a digit,
turning reconciliation into
a fast-food, drive-thru religion.

       three number 2's (lying to parents)
       one number 5 (cheating)
       four number 1's (cursing)

Parents were outraged.
How busy can that priest be,
that he can't hear proper confessions?
What was he doing with his time
that was more important than the
spiritual lives of their children?

The answers avalanched out
in court years later, painfully
clear in the huge number assigned
to his sin in the class action suit.

Destiny of the Modern-Day Gladiola

I kneel in my garden.
Once boasting upright,
tight-fisted buds,
now a carpet of
leaning green stalks
that crush perennial curls
of citrine, vermillion, peach.

Thru generations of crossbreeding
and cultivation, her hybrid flowers,
now more robust and abundant,
quickly bend to the earth.
Beautiful, ruffled blossoms
too cumbersome for
her long, slender stem.

I am told God never gives us
more than we can handle,
and want to believe
that no matter the circumstances,
I will bloom once more.

But as each flower opens,
the mass of a broken heart
pulls me down.

My body in the dirt.
My shriveled petals
pinned to the ground.
Their spirit suffocates
under my burden.

Loaves and Fishes

They talk of their gods,
these women of faith.
Words whispered,
messages received
amidst minutia of daily life
and in grand gestures of
miraculous healing.

A window opens,
sheer curtains flutter
in sweet air,
a green tulip tree leaf
clings to the screen.

I keep looking for a
burning bush, a chance
to put my hand in the wound.
I long to let in the
sunlight of the spirit, but my
windows are painted shut.

When I open the screen door,
the wind slams it closed.

The Wedgewood Nest

They swim in my bowl, baby birds on a milk pond.
Tiny, veined feet work under the surface.

Problems to fish out. I gently scoop each up
with a silver soupspoon. Down drips white.

Yet there in the bottom, an egg that did not hatch.
Cracked open, like a lipoma clinging to the china,

refusing to nudge. The bad egg, the dilemma.
If I try too hard, I'll disrupt it, piece the yolk,

stain the cream a poison, canary yellow.

Rats with Furry Tails

I hate squirrels, all up
in the business of my yard.

Scaling the bird feeder to steal sunflower seeds,
tainting the carefully tended tomatoes,
a single bite out of each ruby heirloom globe,

harassing my dogs,
digging up rows of crocus bulbs,
gnawing their rooted potential,

swinging through my trees,
scurrying under patio furniture,
knocking pumpkins off the stone wall,
joyously splattering them on cement below.

In, out, up, down, back, forth,
frenetic energy, nervous chatter.

A mirror of my
worry and fret,
constantly needing reassurance,
unable to quiet my own thoughts.
Incessant conversation, chronic busyness,
free-floating anxiety.

A wiry squirrel scampers
across my grass,
an acorn in her mouth.
Go away, I think, *go away
and hide your nuts.*

Mantra

I am not daughter
I am not wife
I am not parent
I am not friend
I am not poet

I am only the pure spirit.
Mother energy rises in me.

Free of thought, all my hats removed.
A lotus flower with a thousand
petals blooms from my crown.
I feel the cool breeze of The Divine.

CHRISTENING THE SHIP

Circus Act

She learned to juggle early,
passing the demands
of mother and grandmother
from hand to hand.
An orange and a beanbag,
juggled with one arm behind her back.

But now she is sandwiched
in a five-ring generational circus,
tossing with one fifty-year-old hand,
catching with the other.

The added challenge of
a bowling pin daughter,
whose shape is hard to manage.
The weighty chainsaw of a grandchild
tossed into the arc over her head.

orange, beanbag, bowling pin, chainsaw
orange, beanbag, bowling pin, chainsaw

Juggling for their lives,
she must keep them moving,
never let them touch the ground.
One slip and her Big Top family
will fall apart. The ever-moving
circle allows her no rest, little joy.

If only they would
gracefully trapeze through old age,
independently unicycle into adulthood.
Stop jamming themselves into
cannons and clown cars.

orange, beanbag, bowling pin, chainsaw
orange, beanbag, bowling pin, chainsaw

Failure of her arthritic hand
to make one catch,
divert her eyes for just a second,
and it would all come crashing down.

Piles of fruit, exploded bags of beans.
The chainsaw jumping across the floor,
chipping the bowling pin's enamel finish,
nicking her legs, spraying
fiberglass and orange rind.

Lullaby

Bakelite ashtrays overflowed with Winstons and Kools,
as her parents' friends mingled on a sea of shag carpet,
and swayed to Dusty Springfield on the turntable.

Her mother smelled of White Shoulders,
and her father was the life of the party.
They talked and laughed until the tension was obvious,
and the guests invented reasons to leave.

When the screams and slams and accusations began,
the girl in the flowered nightgown knew to escape. Quietly
pulling a chair across burnt orange tiles, she found the
answer in the sink.

In the bottom of thick crystal glasses, warm swallows of
Brandy Alexander, cherries soaked in Whiskey Sour, a few
sips of a Pink Squirrel.

The key was drinking just enough to feel safe. It worked
every single time, tucking her into a dream of happily-ever-
after, and the only thing she could count on.

Soon the parties stopped, and her parents split, but
it took two more decades for the booze to stop working.

My mother wore a bikini in 1972

and a bathing cap with a fake
ponytail sprouting out the top.

She couldn't swim,
but was she beautiful.

"Better to be envied, than to be pitied,"
she'd chirp,
her blue eyes and high cheek bones
masking the hollowness inside.

When endometrial tissue
seeped from her womb,
and strangled her internal organs,
they scraped her
28-year-old insides clean,
with the nonchalance
of a melon baller
deseeding cantaloupe.

Splattered her uterus
into a metal pan.
Stripped her of the fallopian tubes.
Plucked out her left ovary,
and then robbed her
of her right.

My father was a paratrooper in Vietnam

He trained at a base in God-knows-where, Texas
to parachute out of airplanes,
without landing on cactus,
or the pink stucco hospital, where I was born.

He rescued my teenage mother each evening.
Scared of the scorpions invading our house,
she covered them with shoe boxes
and waited for him to remove the problem.

He flexed his 'Don't tread on me" tattoo
and told how he'd fought off a rattlesnake
with only a penknife – the bravado of
a young man not old enough to buy beer.

He repeated the only rule in our odd world,
"Bite the bullet, all ways, and always."
No crying allowed, but we could throw
back our heads, and howl like the wolves.

When my husband insisted that I tell my parents,
the humiliation was almost unbearable. A hidden
weaknesses that needed to be confessed,
"I just need you to know, I'm sick."

When they reacted, it was almost physical,
obviously struggling for an appropriate response.
"You'll beat it kid," he said, as my mother whined,
"'Why did you wait so long to tell us?"

When we knew damn well, the real question was,
"Why did you have to tell us at all?"
True alpha females put the pack first,
and slink off into the woods, to die alone.

I have him drop me off outside the hospital,
because no parent should have to watch their child
go through this, and I know there isn't a shoebox
big enough to contain my disease.

I feel the sting as the drip enters my vein.
The chemical serpent squeezes my chest –
but the old man can't fight this enemy.
It's my job to win this war, for us all.

I have been trained well, so I tell him I'm fine.
Driving home, he burrows into his olive Saab,
marking his territory with cigar smoke and talk radio,
protecting himself from my nausea and fear.

I bite the bullet, until my teeth crack.
I ignore the metallic taste in my mouth,
as I jump into the free fall of my private hell.
But tearless, Daddy, all ways, and always.

Eleven Weeks

> *Saint Anthony, Saint Anthony, please come around,*
> *something is lost and cannot be found.*

She slides her hands under leather couch cushions,
finds only Cheerios, paperclips, a dime, a Barbie shoe,

dumps out her purse, spreads out the wallet,
shakes it upside down, rips out the satin lining.

She rummages through junk drawers, stuffed with twist ties,
matchbooks, pinking shears, pricks her finger on an open mat knife.

> *Saint Anthony, Saint Anthony, please come around,*

Sweeps her arm under beds, only to find old socks, dust bunnies,
under this bed where the whole thing started and then fizzled out.

Searching for what was gone, what she could not hang onto.
Like it was inadvertently left in a grocery cart, or church pew,

or the jumble of her car trunk. Word on the tip of her tongue.
As simply said as "she lost her car keys" or "she can't find her phone."

> *Something is lost and cannot be found.*

She lies there on the crinkling white paper, thinking of Saint Jude,
patron saint of lost causes, petitions him, champion of the hopeless,

as the speculum enters. The doctor explains the procedure, the how
and why of the D & C, dilation and curettage, expressed as lightly and

breezily, as if it had been overlooked or misplaced, a piece of mail,
a remote, a shopping list, a faded memory, whispers that she lost the baby.

1950 Western Union

> "Dating Americans. Stop.
> Send daughter now. Stop"

My marriage was arranged, long before I was
shipped from the toe of Italy's boot, to a
honeymoon night in Atlantic City, armed only
with a name that was a nod to the Blessed Mother
and an envelope filled with recipes written
in my grandmother's long hand.

His parents had been worried about *Susans* and *Karens*,
Protestant girls who would spread their legs in attempts to
trap their Valentino son. Their boy needed

a wife like me, who could knit and tat, knew the timing
to a perfect pizzelle, would birth fat, olive babies,
live next door, have no friends outside the tribe,
tolerate my husband's bad behavior, and care for
the marriage brokers when they were old.

My 21st century American grandson chose his own wife
from a parade of paramours who didn't know the rosary,
voted pro-choice, and will die having never scrubbed a
kitchen floor on their hands and knees.

A woman who demanded a prenuptial agreement, drug him
across country for her dream job, her daughters as
celebrated as her boys. I stifle envy at her freedom and voice.

But she does not know the arranged security of my life.
Divorce is always an option for her, and a threat.
She worries who will raise her children if she gets cancer.
The au pair, dog walker, and personal trainer will not
throw themselves on her casket when she dies.

When my milk dried up, a cousin served as wet nurse,
her large, soft bosom with her own child on one side
and mine on the other. My own great grandchild will know
only canned formula and plastic nipples.

Grandmother

A platoon of white-coated ants
carries away your fragile breadcrumb body,

leaving a snake pit of wires tangled
by the hollow cicada shell of your bed.

The ambulance speeds from our hive,
like a wasp from the vegetable garden

with a cabbageworm in her mouth.
A worker bee watching my queen die.

Radish Roses

My grandmother taught me,
insert knife in middle and twist
then set in cold water
to allow the bloom.

*Red and white peppermints
individually wrapped in a
a cut-crystal bowl at the funeral home.*

How to prune a rose bush,
float anything in Jell-O,
remove laundry stains with Aqua Net.

I knew I could survive a collapsed lung
because she had survived a
1930's tuberculosis sanatorium.

She taught me that both her sons
should have been at the funeral.
The priest should have pronounced
her name correctly.
My cousin should not have worn jeans.
.
If I ever found myself in an alley
find a bottle and break it.
Carry it shard-end out.

*Her spirit rose in me.
I walked back into the funeral home,
picked up the cut-crystal bowl, dumped
every peppermint into my oversized purse.*

CARGO

The day you were born I grew fangs

and those who dare hurt you, learn to fear my rattle.

I coil through sand, and leaves, and circumstances,
waiting to strike, widen jaws, and consume my prey.

Fat mountains in my snake length.
From the incompetent mohel, who I swallowed feet first,
until the final gulp of his arthritic hand.

To your ex-wife, who I'd waited so long to silence with my poison.

Spiders and toads, mean playmates and critical bosses,
who mistake me for harmless, as I sidewind and snap.

You, my beloved hatchling, are the son of a viper,
because your mother is the daughter of sheep.

The Diameter of the Mouth

The mouth of the bottle is two centimeters across.

We had hoped the math was on our side.
Statistically he would beat the odds and
regress toward the mean, where
two outliers produce something
closer to the median.

Two giants produce a child of average height,
two geniuses' offspring has a normal range IQ.

The mouth of the bottle is two centimeters across,
just large enough for him to crawl into.

Regression toward the mean.
Where two alcoholics produce a social drinker,
instead of someone
lying next to the worm
at the bottom of the bottle.

Carnival Gold Fish Boy

We had the requisite pet parade,
gerbils, hamsters, hermit crabs,
moving from shell to shell,
their naked forms, pale mutant
spiders, like my son, searching to fit in.

I wanted a carnival goldfish boy,
that lives longer and stronger
than anyone could have imagined
despite the odds, content to swim
in the little bowl, not the outlier
always trying to contort himself
into normal people's emotional ponds.

I was unprepared for a toddler correcting
my observation that the "*fluffy*" cloud,
was actually cumulus,
who read *A Wrinkle in Time*
in kindergarten and could do calculus
before he could ride a bike.

My dream boy, a solid bulky form,
a gold crown crooked on his frog head,
strong legs to spring and splash.
The real one hides in deep water,
an overgrown polliwog, squirming
in mud, like a rock with a tail.

My daily prayer the same
since I bought him a zoo in a box,
a vintage menagerie of animal crackers
in a cardboard circus car with a string handle.

Unused to things not electronic,
or neon or dinosaur shaped,
he stared at me blankly and asked,
"What am I supposed to do with this?"

I look down at him, then up to the heavens,
and asked the exact same thing.

Storm Windows

as she decorated the nursery
a panicked tap of praying mantis
tall, proud, hands folded in worship
trapped between two panes of glass

in hormonal bliss
she thought him a good omen
a messenger in preparation
for the arrival of a son

encased in the transparency
he calmed briefly for her to lift the pane,
free him into the world with good tidings
of the beloved infant to come.

———————

proud, grace filled, handsome
hands folded in prayers ignored
trapped between pains of
addiction and self-loathing

smashing into the glass,
panicking when she tries to assist
the beautiful blessing,
she cannot cure

demon trapped within,
keeping him slave to the needle
she finds him puddled on the floor
and prays she can find a pulse.

Checkmate

Her photos of paintings in Lascaux portray hunters and the animals they killed. Her French modern kitchen, painted white, blue, and yellow, holds framed photos of children she birthed.

School portraits on the windowsill overlook her garden – all perennials, white daisies, black-eyed Susans, the purple haze of New York ironweed – pop up year after year, and flourish. Unlike the children, who need constant tending and have incessant demands.

Red-wing blackbirds dot her yard, inky feathers with a splash of scarlet. A checkerboard, but theirs is more a game of chess, a daughter fighting to survive, a mother struggling to help.

A chess player must be able to see the board from both sides, black and white. This demanding girl should be the master, but no one wins.

And since a mother is only as happy as her unhappiest child, she finds no joy in the kitchen or garden, moving back and forth from hunted to huntress. Longing to take red paint and scrawl on the cave walls of her French modern kitchen

THIS IS KILLING US BOTH.

Charlotte's Adopted Son

Trapped
in a tangle of ideas,
and twisted DNA,

you toil under
gossamer strings,
struggling
for structure,
worrying
about the future,
fighting
to save your life.

Holding on
by a thread,
you unsteadily tailor
a world for yourself,
even though
you lack the
words to explain.

Yet crated in
these circumstances,
beats the biggest heart,
the kindest soul.

Know, my child,
I would give
my life
to produce silk
and spin you a web.

Because I know
the love and genius
that rise up
from the pigsty of
a difficult journey.

I would weave
RADIANT,
TERRIFIC,
and HUMBLE
into my web,

insuring that
you would win
first prize.

His Time of the Month

On laundry day, he built forts with warm
white sheets while I fashioned bath towel
capes, granting him super powers.
His first paid job: folding washcloths
and matching his dad's argyle socks.

Later, I did wash during Friday night
boy-girl parties, stomping up & down
basement stairs to announce my presence,
joking that I was not a grandmother because
our clothes were clean by Saturday morning.

We had the inevitable lace bra or thong
mixed in with dirty clothes from college,
my boy, far from unstained, with me as
his wrinkled, static-filled mother. Now
he washes their clothes on weekends,
while she baristas for tips, the young
woman with whom he is building a fort.

As he leans over the sink, scrubbing
bloody yellow boy-cut briefs, I realize he
celebrates every part of her, given the super
power of knowing how to love women, a
cape I saw on the feminist man, with the
argyle socks, I chose to be his father.

I hope he'll leave her stuff in the dryer for me
to fold, the flowered wrappings of this gentle
woman who appreciates my son. "A suggestion,"
 I say, "Use cold water. Warm temperatures set stains."

Lactation

Like pulled taffy, her breasts stretch for thousands of miles.

Pert nipples, once met by gummy smiles
and pearly buds of tiny teeth now sag and crack as
grown children feed them through metal rollers,
twisted emotional wringers, from university to Wall Street.

Staccato claims that they are too busy to talk,
that she always says the wrong thing,
machine gun into her chest,
but within her haggard bosom, her heart knows
they are fragile, fearful of breaking down,
sobbing like babies to their aging mother.

Even when they rally to handle things themselves,
instincts tug her flesh, like a cow ready for pasture,
swollen udders brush against a filthy barn floor.

What budded in youthful anticipation,
blossomed into sweetheart necklines,
produced pure milk for their rosebud mouths,
are now endless wells to take blame, quiet demons.

Her breasts nurse adult children, and in spite of themselves,
although they droop with resentment and loneliness,
continue to rise to the occasion, swell with devotion,

let down milk.

ANCHORED

I am turning 55 years old

softening to mush,
bruised with
muddy liver spots,

my Chiquita yellow
now a mustard hue.

Time to turn me into bread
instead of solitary fruit.
Mix me with flour, eggs, sugar,
form a loaf from which
I can slice myself.

I miss the days
of ripening,
when I hung in a
florescent green bunch,
firm and slightly bitter.

I resent the mellow
maturing of fruit,

a thick piece to
feed my man.
Cushiony and soft,
a tired undressing of what
he once peeled excitedly,
with his teeth.

Aqua Zumba at the YMCA

We are invisible, women of a certain age, between hot and doddering.

We gather at the local pool in one-piece bathing suits, real, ample, pillowy breasts bobbing above the surface. Hips and thighs wiggle, cellulite and stretch marks below choline blue, sturdy feet, corned and calloused. You perch on your lifeguard stand, in a wife-beater and Tommy Bahama board shorts. I watch you smirk, laughing at the old broads gyrating to Nicki Minaj.

But let me guarantee you something, Son.

Forty years ago you would have given your right arm to tap **this**.

Math of the Mom & Pop Shop

They hung out the "Open for Business!" sign a 1/4 century ago. She owns 51%. Her MBA hangs from the wall in a $1 frame.

He reminds her no less than 15 times to get the invoice notarized. He tells her 10 times to send the package Fed Ex not in USPS.

He mansplains how to write a business letter at least once a week. She has only told him to go fuck himself 12 times in 25 years.

Mouth like a Sailor

The type of girl who would steal your wallet,
then help you look for it. Her own parents warned him,
she was not the marrying kind.

Sentenced to a lifetime of apologizing for her when she
drank too much, talked too loud – the over-processed hair,
too short skirts, every word a curse, or a lie.

But time proved him right. His love softened her edges,
taught her to listen. She took vows, kept them,
rose to every occasion,

feathered their nest with classic books and throw pillows,
firewood, cotton-scented candles, and quick-mix cornbread.
Wife, mother, confidante, champion, lover, coach

through decades of in-laws, baby showers, office parties,
late night conversations, surgeries, covered dishes, unemployment,
childbirth, home improvements, midlife crisis, cancer scares.

Men wanted what he had. They both knew that —
but sometimes she caught him staring at her,
when he thought she was asleep.

A look of sadness she understood, because he missed the
filthy mouth and dirty mind, the girl, never ladylike,
always late, who never apologized,

who would tell him to shove his career, his family,
their pain-in-the-ass kids. Screw the civic association,
grandparent day, retirement parties, living wills,

get right in his face, shove her finger into the core
of his chest, and say, "Listen you son of a bitch!
Don't you think I miss her too?"

"Riding Mower $800, Good working condition"

Too big for this small yard, but allowed him to do the grass himself after they replaced his hips, after she threw in the towel on this ½ acre of responsibility

"Riding Mower $600, Good working condition"
Bought when the kids left, a daughter who could mow the lawn in 35 minutes, and the delicate flower son who needed 90, including a break and a snack, like us, a mule and a show pony

"Riding Mower $400, Good working condition"
The 55+ community pays someone to cut the grass. She will no longer need to yell, "Be careful!" out the window. He won't shout back, "Mind your own beeswax, Marie!"

"Riding Mower $200, Good working condition"
Still one step behind the Jones' fancy landscaper, but still able to get the job done. Still in love with this tiny house, big life, long marriage

The veterans come to haul away the donation and give her a receipt for $100
She stands in the road next to the fish-shaped mail box and cracking sidewalk, in front of the starter home, now being downsized, McMansion dreams that never materialized, the beach house that never washed ashore, a condo in the city where another woman lived;

this little house, where she went to bed every night knowing she was put there to love her imperfect, wonderful, old man. She spreads her feet apart, puts her hands on her hips, digs down deep for the moxie and screams at the trailer rolling down the street ---

"IT'S STILL IN GOOD WORKING CONDITION"

Grand Slam

His cane clomps along hardwood
like the tennis ball he bounced
against cinderblock walls in their
first squalid apartment, where they
took each other seriously, for granted,
on the kitchen counter, the sagging mattress.

She slithered through rooms,
her perky breasts and buns, now
shuffle and trudge through their house.
Athletic shoes supporting arches and
balancing a pendulous bustline.

He'd lie in their loft, throwing a yellow orb
against the wall and watch her dress,
sexy as hell morphed into slumped
on the couch watching Wimbledon.
She tucks and conceals,
he ices knees and tennis elbows.

Yet once in a while the ball
swings back into motion. She catches
him checking out her legs, the
thump of his cane, tennis ball
bouncing to the surface,
the clomp, bump, and serve of passion,
and she thinks, "Man, he's got a great ass."

Terrain

she unrolls her body like a
brittle, ancient map

field of pink evening primrose
silvery track of scar tissue

dune of lump biopsy
hidden cave of episiotomy

twisted highways of varicosities
arthritic hands run over land and sea

she curls herself around him
and whispers welcome home

Old Wives' Tale

On a manicured lawn of self-control,
we sit and stand on cue.
My heels sink into the body-rich soil,
as if earth is pulling me
into an ancestral juggernaut.

I want to strip off the Armani suit and crown myself

with the black veil of thick mountain women,
whose gnarled hands pluck grief from my body,
as naturally as pulling olives from a branch.

Thrown back into a choir of peasant dialects,
we kneel against the stony ground.
We rock back and forth in our lament.
We scream, and wail, and pull out our own hair.
In a language I never learned, we shout out for God.

I want to crash your urn onto the mausoleum steps,
crawl thru your ashes, and rake my polished nails
into the graveled bone and tooth.

As if magically I could breathe in the ash,
shove the cinder into my mouth, and bring you back to life.

November 22, 1963

She told her parents it was a stomach virus,
cramping until she passed the locket-sized fetus
and flushed it away, like a carnival goldfish.

They'd thought she was at the library,
when she followed the lady
up a metal fire escape
to a couch covered with a filthy sheet.

She obeyed gruff instructions
to remove underwear and stocking.

The doctor smelled like mildew and gin,
the spaghetti pot filled with steaming water.

She clutched her black patent leather purse
as she laid back, and felt the bile and panic
climb into her throat.

Late that night, she hid the soaked pads
in a Hush Puppies box and smuggled them
to the incinerator.

The apartment rattled with her mother's sobs,
her father's shouts about the injustice of it all.
Tears for Rose's boy and prayers for Jackie.
Not the grandchild washed into the Chicago sewer,
not the daughter who wanted to die.

New York Times, July 3, 1981
"Rare Cancer Seen in 41 Homosexuals"

I remember when sex was fun, before the die of fear was cast. I remember when the diagnosis was an automatic death sentence. I remember watching you shrivel and decay, like a forgotten onion at the back of a pantry shelf. I remember the sound of your laugh, before the ragged cough.

Current Events

Did you hear the pope broke his arm?
He was having breakfast with the cardinals
and fell out of the tree!

Sister Ann said the other children wanted to learn,
and didn't appreciate his inappropriate use of class time.

Not living up to his potential was the mantra
of parents and guidance counselors.

Wasted every day after school
in his best friend's basement.

What a waste!
women whispered,
when they figured out his sexual preference.

So, the irony was not lost on us.

Infectious waste receptacle, red and plastic,
perched on the nightstand.
His precious energy squandered
on a parade of regrets.

When the medication caused his mouth to tingle,
and parasites infested his intestines,
opportunistic infection took up lodging in his throat.

On the 28th day of incessant diarrhea,
the doctor formalized his diagnosis.

10% loss of body weight.
Wasting syndrome.

Emanation

Sister Perpetua told us of the gifts.
Gold, myrrh, and
frankincense,
that burned forth the
scent of heaven.

Now, the putrid air clings to everything.
The stench of soiled sheets and adult diapers.
Latex, and the perfume of antiseptic.
Nurses' perspiration and sweaty thighs
sticking to plastic chairs
that surround the bed.

Even the doctor's voice reeks and oozes.
Words like Kaposi's sarcoma,
oral thrush, and opportunistic infection.

Smelling like cigarettes and anxiety,
we inhale, and force ourselves
to enter his room, and smile.

1996 Man of the Year

AIDS patients from rural Kenya
to San Francisco were
phoenixed from the plague by
Dr. Ho's drug combination.
TIME magazine picked him,
champion of the near dead.

You were chosen to be in the trials,
the newest in a long line of meds,
but you could no longer eat
and the seizures had begun.

One Saturday you gathered us
and asked permission to stop fighting.
We shut off the oxygen, circled the bed,
and layered our voices one over the other,
"Go toward the light Jeffrey, go toward the light."

I wish we'd been braver, more trusting,
but our backbones were crumbling as we watched
you stumble with your cross, again and again.
If only we had known this was not snake oil,
but the gift of 'the Lazarus effect.'

Had we owned a crystal ball,
we'd have knelt by your bed and begged,
"Ignore the light Jeffrey, ignore the light!
You start the cocktail Monday."

Statistics of 9/11

Edward Teller, "father of the hydrogen bomb," wrote:

When you... step into the darkness of the unknown...
one of two things shall happen:
either you will be given something solid to stand on,
or you will be taught how to fly.

A lie repeated over 200 times in 102 minutes.

Alive for the 10-second drop at 150 miles per hour.

No way down since the plane sliced into floors 93 to 98.

A smoky juggernaut.
No hand of god to curb the flames,
no gift of flight.

Tumbling from windows on the
103rd floor
99th
101st.

Bodies folded into origami.
No net or parachute,
no 1,500-foot ladders,
just cement and parked cars.

Human water balloons burst apart,
or crumble intact like bagged ice.

The decision to control destiny
when denied wings.

Survival of the Fittest

My first grade class was at the zoo
the day the earth shattered.
Zookeepers held up
the furry, the foragers, the feathered.

> *Eyes on the side, I hide.*
> *Eyes in front, I hunt.*

We learned owls and rabbits,
predators and victims
while the world burst open.

Had I been called to respond,
would my rabbit-self
have clung to the handrail,
sobbed for them to go on without me?
Burrowed into the smoky stairwell
about to collapse and kill the
firefighter sent to my rescue.

Or could I emerge
as patriot and huntress,
swoop to the back of Flight 93,
and vote to take back the plane?

Rise up, spread hero wings
and help crash the drink cart
into the barred cockpit door.

Push Present

Manicured fingernails
grasp the rail of the
hospital bed.
The air buzzes with
a promise of diamond earrings.

They thank God and Jesus
for answering their prayers.

Ten fingers, ten toes,
"It's a boy" helium balloons,
and powder-blue carnations.

Health insurance pays for
the light box that
shields her jaundiced prince.

Hands press against
the dusty ground,
she delivers the girl into
the cleanest rags she could find.

By the bucket of tainted water,
she prays to pass the cord.

Afterbirth splatters on red dirt,
quickly a bouquet of buzzing flies.

The infant suckles
a starved, milkless breast.

Missionaries say,
"We are all God's children"
but fail to mention that
we are not loved equally.

ABOUT THE AUTHOR

Maria Masington is a poet, author, and spoken word artist from Wilmington, Delaware. Her poetry has appeared in more than a dozen publications including *Adanna, The News Journal, The Broadkill Review, Gyroscope Review*, and *Earth's Daughters*, in addition to receiving recognition from the University of Colorado.

In 2016, she received an honorable mention for a collection of work in the Dogfish Head Poetry Prize. She has also had seven short stories published in both local and international press.

Maria is a member of The Mad Poets Society and is an emcee and featured poet on the local art scene. She has been a guest on WVUD ArtSound and a three-time fellow at the Delaware Division of the Arts Cape Henlopen Poets and Prose Retreat.